Black Night is Falling
Poems by Scott Woods

BRICK CAVE BOOKS
BrickCave.Media
2024

Black Night is Falling
Poems by Scott Woods

All rights reserved
© 2024 Scott Woods

ISBN: 978-1-960105-20-2
All rights reserved. No part of this publication may be reproduced, stored in a retrieval system or transmitted in any form or by any means, electronic, mechanical, photocopying, recording or otherwise without the prior permission of the publisher or in accordance with the provisions of the Copyright, Designs and Patents Act 1988 or under the terms of any license permitting limited copying issued by the Copyright Licensing Agency. No part of this book may be used or reproduced in any manner for the purpose of training artificial intelligence technologies or systems.

Published by: Brick Cave Books
Text Design by: Scott Woods & Bob Nelson
Author Photo by: Joss Ford
Cover Artwork by: Jason Wood
Cover Design by: Scott Woods

BrickCaveBooks.com
2024

CONTENTS

CHAINS AND THINGS

The Ave	2
Day Of The Dead At Bushman's Carryout	4
Pumpkin Seeds	6
Swing Low, Sweet Chariot	7
The Blues Is Your Reparations	9
Before I Let Go	11
This Was a Tape I Wasn't Supposed To Break	14
Bill Cosby Brought Me Into This World But I Have Taken Him Out	15
Muva Drum	18
Psalm For a Woman Who Knows Herself, Chapter 5	20

A BIRD IN THE HAND

Gallery Hop	22
Song For A Razor-Shaped City	23
Fence Shrine #7	26
Autumn Infiltrates the Defense Supply Center	28
Franklin Park	29
Ordnance	31
The Gods You Leave Behind	32
Hey America, Let's Both Get Cancer and See Who Goes First	34
Swole	36
Miss Jane Pittman Has Words With Rachel Dolezal	38

SUN TZU

Peace B. Steele	42
Beckon	44
Mija Woos Forgetting	46
The You Without Poetry	47
A Symphony Of Uncaring	48
Dusk	50
Any Poet Who Says No Is A Liar	51
Last One Given	53
How Poets Say They Love You Now	54

Southern Gal	55
An Act of Black On Black Time	56
Ho'oponopono	57

CAN'T LOSE

Smokestack Lightnin'	60
When All of the Talking Heads In The Blues Documentary Are White	61
Nonsense & Regulation	63
The Car Runs The Underground Railroad Through Bexley, Ohio	66
The Scott Woods I Have Not Friended Online	68
Don't Say Friend	70
What the Men You End Up With Will Possess	73
In Search Of A City	74
Pause	78
We Are So Civilized Right Now	79
Land Acknowledgement	82
The Cookout	84
Notes	87
About the Author	91

i've broken into poetry's house. it smells
unclean/unholy. and there is nothing here worthy of theft

From "Intruder", Wanda Coleman

CHAINS AND THINGS
(B.B. KING)

THE AVE

Surrounded by the gold and pearl sheen of a living summer,
streets paved with shimmering black gold,
a field we call a park that happens to be
where our houses meet and stop to say,
"this is all I need," we do not lose ourselves. We find us.

"We frolickin' out here" is not a question.
We do not declare the frolicking.
We do not aspire to the frolicking.
The run and roll is just how we say Monday here.
We go to our barber and say edge us up,
but leave the grass intact. Where we're headed,
no one is going to care what color our crowns are,
or what we did to earn them.

And because it is summer, never
let it be said the spice was not real.
Licking our fingers after every chip,
red stardust waving us to the bottom
of every foil bag ripped open clean,
the universe telling us it loves us
and we love us and in the us is you,
the perfectly imperfect way of seeing a season
glazed in sweat and grass, glad no one has bagged it.
The world telling us it loves us,
which is not how a universe gets down,
all cosmic and distant, stingy with its embrace.
It is the reason why you capitalize the B now and love it:
all you can ever be was already there the whole time.

So let us to a place where
you claim the streets and the streets
claim you back, no need to earn it.
Claims you for child, nurtures you without charge.
You cannot remember the last time you saw your shadow
on the street's skin, or feared someone else's.

Scott Woods

All blocks are your block, all corners your corners.
Run its fields, share its bags of barbecue chip living,
lie in the placid mist of an answered prayer
until you lose your days.

There is nothing to fear here.
Heaven is too small a word for what we contain.
We can hear the ocean from here,
pounding against the tar beach shore of the 'hood,
a stream of cars turned into wave crush,
the bliss of a love remembered well,
running its wax and wane game against the asphalt.
I promise the sea has no more stories than
an 18-wheeler leaning into a rumble strip.
The rhythm of our kissing in this screen door dark
hits just right, the rush and settle of the freeway
a searching shower of rhythms that never die
in mouths that never cease seeking purchase.
Sea foam kisses every rock, then leaves,
then returns, a prodigal paramour playing
tongue games, unyielding in its love and air brakes.

Turning on sweated sheets into the sound
of midnight waves, I think we made it to somewhere,
but if I'm being honest, I don't even remember
what we were ever running from.

DAY OF THE DEAD AT BUSHMAN'S CARRYOUT

I am Black and this carryout ain't,
so every day could be a day of the dead.

We celebrate it by not covering ourselves,
beaming brightly into security cameras
perched behind counters, vultures with a job,
imploring us to smile, as if that were the photo
they'd show on the evening news
if this juice run goes south.
We celebrate by keeping things as real as possible,
scratching only where we itch today,
showing only the teeth we've paid for,
a grill we cook only gold smiles on.

It is the day of the dead again
But do you know Black people invented the gig economy?
And the girl with the Kendrick tattoo is not
a computer hacker unless you count that autumn
when she bought a cracked firestick in the parking lot
and dropped every spoiler for every show for two months.
All the dollars pinned to her string-top are a wish.
She could buy all the candles in this store
with a bouquet like that if they sold them.
A store that doesn't sell candles in a place
where the lights go out every fifteenth has
trouble on its mind. A beaming halo of bullshits.
You slide her that one you were saving
to become a Now & Later king.
You have no idea who she is spreading wide
across her hips or mourning, or both.

It is the day of the dead again
so make way for the delivery driver's dolly
and the wino and the scratch-off posse
in their work uniforms
already smelling of six o'clock.

Make way for skipping school sex
and fake-out summer nights.
Make way for a petition to tell everyone
to hold up while you call off work.
And the parade honors that:

no cash register ding
no cross-aisle testimony
no whining child who don't know what's at stake.

It is the day of the dead again
and he has found it. Discovered it, really,
for it was only a legend, whispered about
on every block and porch for two miles
amidst a rainbow of gang colors.
He holds it up to the light,
all gasp and dammmmmmn and fist pump.
He has found the bag of Zapp's Voodoo chips
Behind the Grippos that even the owner,
for all his forgetful aisle-dancing we know
is not a dance, did not know was there.
And oh, he talks about how he will pay the extra
twenty-five cents to take it home,
caresses it in his palm, a child made of chip dust,
and for a moment, on this day,
which is really like every other day,
we celebrate him from the bottom of our hearts
and our pockets and our memories
of what a dusty spell tastes like
as he stumbles out the door,
then lash him across his back
for the cheap booze with which
he will wash down such glorious sand.

PUMPKIN SEEDS

If they sold them in March you'd wince in disgust.
Never mind they're out of season.
You just don't see the point, what,
with all these sunflower shells lying around.
Protein is for wimps and hippies,
your brother says, the paragon of health.
One diabetic foot short of a regular parking space,
shaking candy corn in his hand like he needs a seven.

SWING LOW, SWEET CHARIOT

(In honor of the August 5, 2023 Montgomery Brawl, the white folding chair speaks)

I, too, was just doing my job
when Chris stopped sitting on my face,
folded me in half, and started swinging.
His knees cracking, an unfinished waltz
played on popcorn husks in a microwave.
Chris becomes unto like Pop-Pop,
the hot sauce of every cookout flowing in his veins,
hands as heavy as a parked pontoon,
every ancestor awakened in his soul and his wrists.

Being a white chair, I wondered if my chance
to do a right and just thing would ever come.
Is this all of that DEI training I've been hearing about?

How many times a chair should have been the answer:
lunch counter stools. Colored bus seats. Mississippi church pew.
All brawls waiting to fix history.

A brawl extends as far as the dust settles.
Ain't no lines in a brawl until the cops come knockin'.
If you're in the middle of a brawl,
you aren't a white woman anymore; you're a brawler.
The fact that you can't brawl doesn't mean you don't get hit.

The trembling thug tears of Chris' ancestors
flowing through him with every summertime
field-hand swing of my body, driving railroad ties
into a Montgomery dock swarming with revenge.

The power of Chris compels you,
white man in white shirt doing white shit.
The power of Chris compels you,
bird-chested white boy looking for trouble.

Black Night is Falling: Chains and Things

The power of Chris compels you,
woman in red dress trying hard to look like surprised.

My cousin is an armchair.
He gon' tell me, had it been the other way around,
nobody would be celebrating.
La-Z-Boy: right there in his name and his thinking.
That fairy tale used to be on postcards
sent 'round the countryside to friends.
Not a chair in sight under the noose.

Moving furniture is not just reserved for arguments.
We are so much more than Saturday night spades table flips.
Using me as a revolutionary act of ancestral recall is,
According to law, a misdemeanor disorderly conduct charge.
If freedom wind blows Alabama way again,
one could serve that kind of time with community service.
Except Chris already did his community a service.

Rosa Parks' bus seat is my cousin,
and one day we'll both be in the Smithsonian,
Legs out, back straight,
save for that one dent in my cheek
where fucked around met found out,
had a baby and called it justice,
It is a constellation that still has a strand
of crying hair stuck to its North Star.

THE BLUES IS YOUR REPARATIONS

There are 10,927 blues songs
about a man done wrong
by a scandalous woman
who bends over pool hall tables
snaking the life out of a man's
paycheck every Friday night,
laughs in his face at his thug tears,
snaps her neck as she walks out
a door he's still paying for,
coos his wallet away from him,
leaves him to rot in jail for
busting in on her and a drummer
from the local juke joint.
A drummer for god's sake.

10,927 songs are about this.
The other two blues songs are about
liquor and food, in that order.

The blues is what you get instead of a check.
Hope you play good 'cause they docked you
five decades for civil rights out the gate.
If you want a raise, die harder.

I saw you try to take 'em off the table
while we wasn't looking, hand caught in the jar.
How you think we got here,
playin' for nothing but more questions:
Can I touch your hair?
Do you do private parties?
Do you dance too?
Do you shuck?
Do you know how to stay quiet?
How do you swallow your blues?
Homemade blues. Organic blues.
Artisanal blues. Got a tap room for these blues.

Put a spigot on the back of a Black man's head
until his spirits are dry.
Aged blues. Seasonal blues. Craft blues.

The blues is what you get instead of a revolution.
Hope your instrument's in tune.
Blues is funny that way.
We have always done more with less.
We have made beds in which we never lie,
planted trees we may one day swing from.
Even the acorn is not our friend.
Johnny Appleseed is the god of lynchings.

The blues is what you get instead of a god,
instead of free lunch, instead of justice.
The blues is what you get instead of a grocery store,
instead of a president, instead of a Second Coming.
The blues is what you get instead of tax abatements,
instead of home, instead of a civic organization.
The blues is what you get instead of a job
because the blues is your job.
The blues is what you get instead of benefit of the doubt,
instead of a working taillight pass,
instead of a proper prayer flung North
that knows where my heaven is.

The blues is your reparations.
Don't spend it all in one place.

BEFORE I LET GO

(For Frankie Beverly)

You can tell by the way her lovers fought
over her casket, carried through Cairo's streets,
that Umm Kalthoum was the most ecstatically adored
singer of all time, grinding poem into prayer,
businessmen rending their suits in the ripple
of the unending desert oasis that was her heartache,
which was every heartache they have ever caused,
which was every heartache
until all that was left was the reaching handkerchief
dancing at the end of her arm
and the end of the stage
and the end of her life
and the end of a record that never fades
and never stops, rocking a needle arm into
a single euphoric spiral groove of vinyl crackle.
All her songs are joy and pain.

Somewhere along the way,
between the cookout and Essence Fest
Frankie Beverly started giving white folks
the business between songs.
Not that they noticed.
Ain't a lot of pumpkin spice between
my man Sidney's smoker and the Superdome.
All of these reports came to me secondhand
from the worried mouths of respectable Negroes,
concerned that somewhere between
"Happy Feelings" and "After the Morning After",
recipes might be loosed, the kitchen within
which Frankie cooked closed for business.
More businessmen tearing at their all-white leisure wear.
What did you think "Joy and Pain" was about?
A rubbed and dusted barbecue rib is the joy.
Whispering when you say white folks is the pain.

Black Night is Falling: Chains and Things

It is not summer until he sings,
and when you hear him off-season,
it is summer wherever you are.

Frankie Beverly is gone
but before I let go, I must tell you
how you sang up under a woman's smile for me,
lifted what I could not on my own.

Before I let go, I must tell you
how my brother who gave you to me died,
how his heart shined too bright one night,
his head become pillow for the floor,
and that even when he went back to the church,
he kept your golden times close to his truck stereo.

Before I let go, I must tell you
that I know the maze's secrets:
that you can only enter
through the index or middle finger,
either pointing or condemning.
I know too that there is no escape.

Once in hand, Frankie Beverly holds you
in something that looks like a fist,
that clutches you, but does not knock the dust
from your summer wings.
He knows you got places to go.
He's going that way, so he carries you.
You don't even care what minotaur might be
stalking that labyrinthine palm.
You only know you are not alone,
that whoever is pounding at the loving casket
of a Black hand that knows its way around
microphone and grill is most likely
a lover playing at pallbearer
responsible for the procession of hustle and grind

that made you put that record on.

Frankie Beverly warned you about them ones
that only want to crawl into that silk-lined maze
beside you, nose in crooked neck,
curled up in barbecue smoke and good sin.

Even then Frankie Beverly is carrying you,
even though we all know it's his turn,
carried through the streets like a pharaoh,
Hannibal crossing Jordan astride a wave of
white cotton and linen love that refuses to let go.

THIS WAS A TAPE I WASN'T SUPPOSED TO BREAK

(Ekphrastic to a photo of a powwow dancer, "Whirling Away" by Inga H. Smith)

I do not know if she brings
the storm in her swinging limbs
or sends it away. The ebb of thunder
in my chest says "yes" either way.
I want my oppression to have dances.
Not the warding off kind,
but the sort that sorts things out,
that brings my blue ancestors out
of their Nelsonville coal mines and
second marriages, that turns
into a dervish at the mere mention
of a man where an apple should be.
I want to know if the prayer is an ecstasy
or a cure because where I'm from
it cannot be both.
We both know a storm when we see one.
I am all thunder, she, all lightning.
All of her songs live off the land
and so do mine.
All of my poems cornrow their hair
and I never have to tell her what that means.

Scott Woods

BILL COSBY BROUGHT ME INTO THIS WORLD BUT I HAVE TAKEN HIM OUT

Lying on the floor of a living room
in front of a stereo built like a sarcophagus
Bill Cosby taught me that my mother
had a laugh reserved for non-saint situations.
I have been chasing that hymn ever since.

Bill Cosby taught me what football was;
showed me why whuppins were not the end
of a conversation but the beginning of a relationship
whose love you will not fathom and I cannot explain;
When I failed college, I let down my mother
and Bill Cosby, in that order

Bill Cosby taught me to love myself the way
white people love me: as subject matter.
The way they love jazz: imperialistically.
The way they love mammy cookie jars: devoutly.
I love myself like mammy cookie jars
stuff myself with they sweetness
smile, never let on that I have smeared
every one of these cookies with this servant tongue.
Bill Cosby has taught me to be a better slave.
Pick the whole field clean with all your teeth.
Bill Cosby is the greatest actor of our generation.

Bill Cosby is dead to me so soon
to when it was going to happen anyway
that I can't even get it up to grieve.
The Bill Cosby I see now is mist-eyed,
a zombie, is not the teacher I have known
The realest monster I have ever let into my home.

Bill Cosby showed me junkyard genius,
how a bedspring could become a harp
if you touch it just so,

how a radiator could be an accordion,
a swollen belly drummed like a timpani,
how the anything of nothing
could become everything to anyone.
Bill Cosby taught me the funkiest scat ever uttered,
a hickey-burr turned to gibberish
in my mind as if it has been clouded
guilty of nothing more than thirst.

Where there is smoke there is fire.
Where there is a forest fire there is a teacup.
I would cast every album onto the flame
if it would give me back my Fat Albert Saturdays.

Bill Cosby taught me how to tell this story:
drop a little of this, take on a little of that,
be a little drunk off yourself.

Somewhere Bill Cosby is buying NBC
to make a television show about
all of the women he must adore,
whose pitch is that he has a different wife
each week with the same name
that he wants me to believe he loves for her mind.
And it's a hit. Bill Cosby has done it again.
Bill Cosby has recaptured Thursday nights,
made it a holiday again. Football Sunday special.
And as we celebrate the golden touch
of America's favorite dad he pours me coffee
and my mind is telling me no
but my body is also saying I'd rather not.

Bill Cosby is dead to me, and I have spun
every groove of every record for any truth,
found him wanting, found myself letting go,
found myself wishing my mother
and I had just talked for once
instead of listening to a record

of someone we could never know,
pretending it was a better teachable moment than love.
My mother and I have said nothing about Bill Cosby
since all of his jokes have died on the vine.
It's as if she's gotten divorced all over again,
another plate disappearing from the table.
I think I am a good son for saying nothing.
Bill Cosby taught me that too.
Bill Cosby taught me that silence is innocence,
that if no one can say a thing then it didn't happen.

Bill Cosby taught me that where there is smoke
there is a woman running into the street
who does not know her name anymore
and who wishes, more than anything,
to be thirsty again.

MUVA DRUM

Water took my woman away,
stomping out on the top of a cresting tsunami
in gold thigh highs and a moving neck,
or leather boots and a moving neck,

or Adidas with fat laces and a moving neck.
Left me outside of a furniture store that used to sell organs,
but still kept the old twenty-foot lyre in front,
as if Pan had come through the hood one day and,
exhausted, laid his harp down and his hooves up
on a 2-for-1 mattress sale sign.

I could not hear anything over the rush
of the wave that came crashing down
except the click of her low heels, turning on blacktop,
crunching away through gravel to the bus stop.

I almost drowned on Lockbourne that day,
so there is nothing you can tell me about water
that I didn't know coming out of the womb.

And when the waters rose again
and they came for the houses, I did not care.
She didn't live in them anymore.
She had taken her gold or boots or laces
She had taken her diaries and New Edition posters
She had taken her albums and swinging barrettes.
And when the jealous sea swallowed me whole
for the second time, I let it kill me.
There is nothing you can tell me about water
that I didn't know coming out of the tomb.

To say she walked on water would be a bridge too far,
but she did walk over my grave once.
I could feel it under my skin, a muscle
warping love that would not let go.

When she saw me again I was mostly undead.

I could hear her drum coming a flood away,
as if she were dancing on the deck of an ark,
hollowed of its pairs and burden,
echoing through the halls of my gut
where a home used to be.

PSALM FOR A WOMAN WHO KNOWS HERSELF, CHAPTER 5

1. Lawd, I love myself more than you could ever show.
2. You turn from me but that's for show. The strands you left on my cheek tell me so, prove you trickster god.
3. Lawd, mark me an acolyte of every nap the heat has not yet pressed to skin.
4. Close all the gates and their pearled bars you like; I'm already inside of you.
5. Lawd, show me all of the ground. I have spent my entire life in the sky. Even when I fall I do it like it's optional.
6. It is the ground which speaks to me. All that dirt I have in my blood but ain't never touched.
7. My face turning into the sun, I go gold, then brown, then fall. And then, I will kiss the earth for the first and last time at once.
8. Lawd, I got wings the color of gasoline rainbows shining through dusty section eight windows. I been stained glass refracting all your glory anyway.
9. I been floating over all this hell already; been so high I even brushed up against you once.
10. Lawd, save me from these secondhand cocoons, from losing myself. Been my own guardian angel for so long.
11. I just wanna be myself with you, and if you can't take me like that, even with all this love, well.
12. Let's just say, I ain't the one fittin' to burn.

A BIRD IN THE HAND
(ICE CUBE)

GALLERY HOP

Handcuffed to an art car
protesters get the valet treatment
from police while firemen
stand to the side, studio assistants
unfolding a white sheet
to hide their work,
an exhibit coming soon,
once the clay has formed
under the running stream of pepper spray
or tears or the spit that comes
with the yelling command,
the whole of High Street a gallery,
a silent auction,
every piece sold out,
Bull Connor painting a master's piece
from beyond the grave.

SONG FOR A RAZOR-SHAPED CITY

First, we require earth.
We were imported wholesale from a land of big skies,
the shipping and handling a caress of waves and whips
prices hung on our toes like body tags,
a distant cousin's belly for bubble wrap,
we cannot drink water without wanting to
drown a 400-year-old song in our throats
that sounds like Marvin Gaye
singing the National Anthem after
crying in a locker room,
needing to kneel,
not yet knowing that one day
that will be an answer.
No place to put those knees, those tears, that water,
so it hits the ground in buckets of song
and dance
and run
and play
and die,
so earth –
ground that doesn't move or sway or rock or flow,
that swallows all memories and bones equally,
the entire democracy of sins –
earth, my dear city, is a non-negotiable.
Do you realize how much land it takes to make the blues?
How many acres of cotton,
plots of shotgun shacks,
rentable plantation getaways you have to
square cubically
then multiply
by the dead root of an oak tree
minus a noose,
carry the dead,
divide family,
use an inverse sin function
raise sweat to the power of whip

take the log of a coon hunt
hit the integer button on an abacus
with skulls for beads,
parentheses humanity
store humanity
recall humanity
fraction humanity
equals a lot of land.

Somewhere in there someone called it blues.
Skipped all the other obvious colors.
Could have called it reds for blood,
browns for skin
purples for bruise
blacks for night.
Someone skipped blacks for night,
went straight for blues.
Bypassed all that stygian firmament with its twinkling naps
teeming with prayers and manifestos and jambalaya recipes
and instead cast their eyes to the body lying
next to them in a cabin,
the moon somewhere else but leaving behind just enough
midnight luster to read the braille of scars on a lover's back,
the shine – such as it was – gone indigo
on her crossing peaks.
And when she was taken,
he went back to the night as if it were an altar,
lay on his bed of straw and lice and empty,
felt her runaway scars still under his fingertips,
each a poltergeist flipping his insides in despair,
then put a fiddle bow to it.
Named it after dem scars, after her.
Dem blues.

You don't even want to see the math on gospel.
We might've done jazz with a backyard back when,
and the real estate footprint of hip hop is enormous!
So sure, you live in a city, but it's a razor-shaped city,

Scott Woods

Got us standing on an edge that's cut us so many times
we just keep dancing through the tears.
A city that puts your name in lights as it cuts your electricity.
Shoots you a block away from a park named after
someone who swears they care,
every grass in it a blade shaving away
resistance like a soul grater.

FENCE SHRINE #7

I invent the places where I want to live
and adorn the plots where I wish to die.
Lafcadio Hearn is out here inventing New Orleans
and I am constantly having coffee with
a neighborhood that has forgotten itself.
I used to be better at this,
used to care more, or maybe it was less.
I used to care less.
I used to be able to walk the street
and be scared of it. There was a living in that.
Now, I can't wait to be swallowed whole.
If you mugged me right now I'd laugh
in you and your gun's face.
I know you didn't bring a knife to a building permit fight.
Can't take this city seriously.
I live in an unserious place.
Too easy not to die here.
I ain't looking to, but I'm saying,
I invent the places where I want to live
and adorn the corners upon which I wish to die.
All your boss level villains are soft.
This city is full of pillows.
All the bags you chase got legs.
You ain't got the wind to catch all these bags they giving.
Give me a body bag.
Stuff it with money if you must,
If it makes you feel better.
All I'm gonna' do is spend it on
good poetry and Umm Kulthum records.
Kick all the North Market dirt you got onto this body.
It ain't that serious. I live in an unserious city.
Even when they kill us they kill us weak.
Predictable violence, a bruise you can see coming.
All they punches telegraphed.
All they bullets clear.
The only surprise is the justice you pretend to serve.

Scott Woods

I live in an unserious place.
Can't take this city seriously.
And I'd be rolling all over this floor
if it ever learned how to tell the joke right.

AUTUMN INFILTRATES THE DEFENSE SUPPLY CENTER

Steel fencing
on the other side
a shock of red bouquets
guards a still-green torso
shielding autumn
from its lush memory.

A birch of perfect resilience
fireworks stashed
in its summertime jaws.
Standing post
next to a beige warehouse
in the morning sun
Like all battles it is brilliant
and hard to watch.

A life not so much planted
as commandeered
both belonging
right where it is
and still, more beauty
than that place deserves.

FRANKLIN PARK

You have been all my autumns
I longed to escape into you
during every summer school,
a wild child lost to the rusted grills and
sweat of tall grass laid to the side.

When this city makes me feel like an insect
you are my anthill.
Your ducks are notoriously gangster.
I make chocolate angels in your dust where
you did not grow this season.
You always a park to me, baby.

Your pond only so deep but
enough I can always see myself.
Promise I was looking for you.
Narcissus of the East Side, my eyes
only catch on your rippling face.
I'm not that pretty.
You know I could never know myself that way
so long as you sitting across from me,
every house along your hip of streets a welcoming.
That's a whole avenue you wearing.
Anybody ever tell you that you look like a downtown?

Every grill master and baby blanket carpet
sings your praises,
the way you hold us,
the way you whisper into our ears
the way you make Broad Street disappear
until Monday morning.

I feel like this could be over sometimes,
we breaking up without saying it out loud.
I have seen you pretend at happiness with another.
You cut them out of the pictures so I can't see

Black Night is Falling: A Bird in the Hand

the encroachment, over bulldozer din,
but your eyes give them away.

Do you remember the back door festivals,
every illegal Martin/Malcolm/Mandela t-shirt,
and how we shot our prom pictures
in your concrete rings and trellises?

I only call you when things is good.
You only listen when things are bad.
I have been an amazing lover but a poor giver.
You my favorite country club,
your ancient trees swaying in the middle
of this battlefield of tar and money.

The clouds that pass over say what's up.
Of course they can see the growing distance
between us every season.
This city is coming for you and I'm too poor to stop it.
Swear they gonna' treat you right this time.
They can bury you in all the flowers they want
but I have not forgotten you the Juneteenth years,
no matter who shot first.

I pray, at the curling smoke altar of every cookout,
that it is not too late, that there is still
a duck feather dipped in gold
where the sun sets on your hips and knolls.

ORDNANCE

None of this is what was promised,
but then the promise wasn't made to me,
so only some of that is fireworks.

Nothing patriotic about the firework in a 'hood.
It commands the same neck-turn we conduct
from rattling trunks of bass.

That's my soul in that crackling willow.
Acknowledge the blood I have spilled
into the inky summer night,

an electric inkblot of ashen freedom
cast back to stars that have always
known the long and moonlit way home.

When we run out of dust we blast
lead into the belly of the sky,
heat poured into summer's black blanket.

We know better than most such tears
in the firmament must come back to us,
the beginning of a soft rain after thunder,

a metal rain whose spittle must come
to rest in some roof, some stoop,
some soft hole you forget we may have to pray over.

THE GODS YOU LEAVE BEHIND

The true romance of the Western
is that farm hands have so many chores
because everything on the land
is always trying to die.

Nobody is writing Dune poems
because we already have a bible.
We already have a book of psalms
and prophecies and it is working
it is working and it is working
and it has twice as many knife fights.

And the water is the blood
And the spice is the flesh
And the worms are the people
and nobody is writing Dune poems
because nobody loves a prophet
that can speak for themselves.
We prefer our gods quiet
so that we might sell you
what the cosmos thinks.

Everything on the land
is always trying to die
is what we tell ourselves
when the land stops bending to the will
of the gods we create.

I don't know who you've been praying to
but my god breaks hard bread over soft heads.
Those other gods, the ones
that make sense and sentience, are gone.
Probably retired to an orchard
where every apple and pear fights to live,
and the sand is just sand
and the spice is just maple bourbon salt

and the worms are just the churning mill
of old gods we left to dust.

HEY AMERICA, LET'S BOTH GET CANCER AND SEE WHO GOES FIRST

Talking to white people about racism
is like telling people that you know how you will die:
no one wants to hear that noise.

People hate to hear you say you know how you will die
because they think you're jinxing yourself,
as if cancer were a Ouija option,
a malevolent strain of cells with googly eyes
and a lolling tongue shoved between the slick
and knowing Western sun and a constipated moon.

I can't remember the last time someone told me
how they were going to die and that's what happened.
No one has ever said – and this has been scientifically
proven – "I'm going to die from a car accident"
and was then struck down by a Ford Escort by lunch.

Despite my keen tradition of failure in this area,
the math here isn't difficult:
Everyone in my family dies of cancer.
It is a condition so thorough I cannot fear another death.
My father died of cancer, and young.
Both of my grandmothers. My grandfathers on both sides.
All of my aunts. Several uncles.
We are quietly running bets on the first cousin
to reap what our genes have sown.
I used to be terrified of flying,
all the turbulent pitches grinding me into prayer
I had not the gods to deliver them to.
No matter how long and rough the ride,
I know cancer will meet me in the terminal.

Talking about racism with certain people is like that.
No one wants you to bring it up,
as if silence was the frost that brings the ivy-creep of

mistaking me for the other Black guy here to a crawl.
People who don't want to catch what you have
would prefer you stay home from work that day
if you're going to come in with racism on your breath.
The only people who enjoy talking about it
are other survivors, comparing break room scars
and microaggression high scores:
"I had two Beckys and a Chad last week."
"Man, I caught a Driving While Black right after I got mistaken
for a co-worker who retired two years ago. And he was Indian."

We know all the shortcuts, speak at least three of the languages,
know all of the grits recipes, can debate the merits
of things only seen on the carry-out spectral scale.
There is a comfort in knowing your devils.
This is why I miss half of what you say:
I am considering what to wear to my next racism debate,
which treatment is most effective to ending this conversation
with as little pain as possible,
and if I will have an appetite when it is over.

There is a comfort in knowing how you will go,
how all of your people go, and standing in that line;
in knowing what the throb in your gut is,
and how talking about racism with someone
who can walk away from it
like a room in which they have flipped a switch
is almost just like that.

SWOLE

I am not stepping on the flag.
I am wiping my feet.
It is uncouth to drag all this America into a house.

Another day done, the half of me that remembers
the Southside Fish Market bursts out of my suit,
While the rest of it is still paying the bills.
I tried respectability but it fit me like a cheap suit.
Could never get the bullets out of my teeth,
Even when I spent all day picking them with nightstick shards.

Swollen from all of the hugging I do.
All I have ever done is lift someone when their God did not answer.
The cathedral you have trapped me in has a Samson moment coming.
Why you think they put pillars in here?
They know I'm a sucker for a flex.

It is uncouth to drag all this America into a house,
and even this busted bald eagle knows it,
its dome melting under the heat of all this truth.
If you scoffed at kneeling football players
you're gonna' hate me.

I got all these seconds in my pocket:
second class citizen
second nature
second wind
second in line trying to get to second to none.

The worst part for you is that I'm not even the first one.
My daddy was bigger than I was, and his daddy before him.
And we all know what it looks like when we
hold our fists in the air, which is to say,
I been catching fireflies during the kiss of dusk and twilight
my entire life, and you can't prove otherwise
unless you can pry my hand open.

So go ahead. I dare you. Take my hand in yours
and try to open it with anything other than love.

MISS JANE PITTMAN HAS WORDS
WITH RACHEL DOLEZAL

Well, speaking as a fictional construct,
let me tell you, America ain't exactly known
for reading the footnotes. I will have to
remember that one next time a coon hound
comes running, death in its spit, skin of
the last wild buck fresh under its claws. I will say,
"Down boy! Heel! You sniffin' at a social construct!"
Send him on his way.

I hear you do hair. Got any recommendations
for when Jesus' blood come running
out your skull hot from a gun butt?
What gel might lay this runaway kitchen
to the side and make a mansion of it?
What product you suggest for when plantation sun
has eaten away your edges, winter your toes,
spring your man, fall your babies?

Ain't none of this about what you think black is.
It about what black catch.
Folks say it shouldn't matter. And yet,
this persists. You persist. That hair persists.
It ain't 'cause I like running in the dead of night
through swamp and wood and buckshot smoke.
I would love me even if you gave me no choice.

But you give me no choice.
Heard you used to rub mud on yourself
so you could play black as a child.
Heard you used to read your grandma's
National Geographics because fantasizing
about being a black person from Montana was a stretch.
I'm not convinced you know I never existed.
I'm certain enough you know less what it mean
to be a black woman than the man wrote this poem.

How come all your role models is fiction?
How come they exotic, unable to be debated with?
Pressed flat into history but never beside you at the march?
You changed your name, Nkechi Amare Diallo,
which means "gift from the gods" in some language
I no longer remember. In what tongue I got it means,
she who sends noose to herself in the mail
she who calls cops to scene when going is not tough enough
she who wants black experience delivered to her door

Trans-black used to be when you crossed state lines
by summer stars until they winked out in the sun,
when you passed for white to stay alive,
not black for Negro scholarships.
Somebody mighty thirsty told me you might be
one of the good ones. Almost spit out all the water
I drank from that "whites only" fountain,
and in 60 years of I ain't never let that water go.

Blackness be a lot of things up and down the line,
but let me tell you what it don't, young lady:
Blackness don't wash off into a shop rag.
It don't come in bags. It don't got receipts.
It could be bought but ain't ever on sale.
It don't take no days off, got no rest in its bones.
And trust me when I tell you,
Life for me ain't been no bottle of bronzer.

SUN TZU
(SA-ROC)

PEACE B. STEELE

Carved our revolution into a marriage,
put hands on it, spun it into the shape
of a useful thing, something
that would hold all this love and pessimism forever.

Unfurling a crown to the roots white meat deep,
all that sore-cheeked momma cooking grace that knows
all of my hungers and none of my beasts.
Each other's everything under our nails.
The songs we make in the kitchen live in our hair;
maybe they breathe, maybe they just sound right.
Either way, there is a racket of bullets in our hearts.
It be New Year's Eve every time we hug.
We a ground pop in case we get asked later.
Got to get our stories straight, even at the cookout.

I want to make this movement moment about you
but there is already so much us in everything:
The click of your tongue at bad jokes lives in my ears.
The rustle of my hair besides yours is an autumn
in which nothing fades or falls.
Some weeks your braids make a kissing chamber,
others I worship in the haze of an afro like the sun.

You keep your heart loaded like your mouth.
I done caught so many strays, I get to say
you put the sass in assassin.
Keep your finger on the trigger of me.
I sorely want to burn anything you aim me at.
Make a national holiday out of my body, baby.
I ain't doing anything right with it anyway.

I see in the back of your mind that you think safe
is soft and want no parts of it.
So I'll make you a deal:
We sign on to love forever,

Scott Woods

knowing forever is as long as it gets,
but with all this sharing just begun,
forever will have to do.

BECKON

I have been on my back so long
every ceiling bears a horizon.
Counting stars in the holes of their tiles,
the constellations I have composed
from the moles of your neck, your belly,
your incense scars.

The sky I am pining for is a summer dusk
eclipsed by your breasts, and the shroud
of your nightfall hair as you lean
into me from above.
Our fingernails cricket song against teeth,
sheet against stones
in the earth of your moans.

Whoever left this window open tonight
was a genius. That car alarm
will forever be our song.
I will pray for you, watch the stars
form over your shoulder, naming their paths
in the tongue of ancestors
you didn't even know you had:
the herb man, the DJ spinning,
the lover who paints with words.
Ruin this canvas for everyone
who comes later. I will pray for you.
I will wait for you to dry.

I have a woman who loves me so much
she can't see me anymore knocking around
in my head, a canary's skull song.
I'm not trying to find the words anymore.
This hip bone altar speaks for us now.

We are supposed to be better than this,
as if we are not our best in this room,

sometimes sun worshipping,
sometimes heathens for dusk.

Our trophies cast into the blackening sky
float the way a good memory should,
constellations out of your scars, your swing,
your lifting breast, your belly gone valley

I am afflicted with a gene of loneliness,
set softly in the womb, a happiness for longing.
I never knew what the word meant
until you did it to me

MIJA WOOS FORGETTING

(For Yoon Jeong-hee)

disappearing isn't what it used to be.
So many whiffs left behind, the couch ripe with
your hair oil, the ottoman a wrestling ring of feet luchadores.

when the traces of autumn fade,
you will sit with yourself as if in recital,
a pavane of toe glissandos that know no winter

you will sit with me until
        the sabotage of forgetting wrecks my letters
you will sit with us until
        the remembering is a bath of quiet sunset kisses
we stopped looking for somewhere along the way
an eclipse becoming a constellation

i will not let you go until you can see this memory
the sunset tongue-red, a carryout cherry stick licked,
because we forget these things

i will not let you go until the leaf burn fills
our throats, the leaving sun pirate gold,
because we bury and lose these things.

i will not let you go until the sunset is a backseat song
sung intentionally out of key, and shaken windows
and the begging hymns memory sometimes takes for granted.

THE YOU WITHOUT POETRY

is not much of a thinker.
Smokes three times what you smoke now
to compensate for all of the things
she cannot see in her mind.

Sees a rose's thorn as a challenge
Took that fireman job and still didn't do
anything with the 2 days off.
Lives the life you want but wants the life you have

Is scared to not know everything,
Is scared of the unknown
Sees the bus as a jungle and not a buffet,
Which is to say, they metaphor wrong

Doesn't wrestle with genocide at all.
Actually, that is the You With Too Much Poetry.
The You Without Poetry wrestles with minutiae
and pretends a cubicle is a crime against humanity.

Sees a dancing plastic grocery bag
but spears it for litter,
cannot take it as the wind trying
to clarify her wishes before answering.

Wants to end it all but cannot find
the words for the letter, so takes things slow:
the bottle, the fattened line in reflection,
the mute boredom of every Tuesday morning.

A SYMPHONY OF UNCARING

All of the things we have planted to keep you away:
Park benches with the rude middle arm of sit-upright
Concrete daggers set in stone where you might seek our help.
If we keep you standing you may move on
to more restful pastures.
A symphony plays outside a hotel to keep you from under its arches
as if there is no way you could possibly love Mozart too,
no way the strings hum sweetly in your ears.

Every poem about you talks like the seasons are wallpaper,
the pillow of autumn leaves, the blanket of winter.
I only ever want to see you in a room like this,
sitting at a table set for you while you can smell
The centerpieces for yourself.

Is it ghosting if you can see them?
If you avert your eyes in the face of the cupped hand?
Is it ghosting if you ignore the asking?
If you suddenly go blind at the sight of a sign?
Who then haunts who, at that bridge between
where you're headed and where they've been?

Projection is a powerful drug, and everyone
on this sidewalk is on it.
The song goes, a house is not a home,
and I guess technically that's true.

If they loved Mozart they wouldn't play that.
You don't use something you love as an engine for inhumanity.
I hope they play your jam by accident.

All of the things we say to keep from helping you:
We know how you'll spend it,
like everything we buy is so precious and affirming.
Anything you spend it on I have bought a hundred times over.

Is it ghosting if you can hear them?
The story they must tell for your largesse?
The tale that makes the giving tree loosen its fruit?
Is it ghosting if you look like me,
And I turn away because but for the grace of God go I?

Is it giving if I feel absolved? If I cry?
Is it giving if I mean it? Is it giving if you thank me?
Is it giving if I make conditions? If I wash my hand quick?
Is it giving if someone sees me do it?

Can I learn to give? Can you teach me to give?
Can I give and not keep score? Can you teach me care?
Can I give when I'm off the clock? Can you teach me shelter?
Can I give and ask you to come back tomorrow,
as you are, ready for more truth between us?
Can I give and look forward to it?
Can I give of myself?
Can I see the symphony of your existence,
which is to say, can I see the symphony of our existence?
How your cello sits by my violin?
How we both laugh at the piccolo player?
How the conductor of all of this is love?
Can I ask you what you want for once?
Can you teach me the right notes to this gospel we sing
of giving?

DUSK

She told me I was beautiful.
I wanted to know what horrors she had seen
that would make her believe that.
Back then I did not have the words,
no standard to fly over her as she passed,
snapping kisses in its flapping wake.
I raked the yard of her back, shedding it of dead love.

I live in dusk made of the color
of sun blush when it laughs, then dies.
It is one of a dozen covenants here,
candle and sheets math. Has weight here,
skies possessing tongue and meat.
When dusk smiled here the room striped,
made a manuscript of runes on her cheek.

We had gone deaf to the songs I set aside.
Sienna was our jam, and scarlet, and cricket song.
Sheets smitten like papyrus, your throat
where the sun dips, chills, shudders.
She made a pelt of my whispers, wore it smooth,
our legs a skein of orange peels and cherry limbs.
No one has said it to me since.

ANY POET WHO SAYS NO IS A LIAR

Have you ever had your heart broken,
she asks, knowing the answer,
and I'm on it before the question mark
hits the air.

I have stitched my loves across every entrance,
petals dropped from the budding embouchure
of every kiss lining the doorways
into me like pinched salt spells.
Whispers pool in bottle tree sigils
I keep like a wine cellar in the sun,
each a chamber to a stilled heart
that remembers how I took
every limb for my own once,
every whistling regret an anthem
to a country found in their leaving laughter.

A refugee on every tongue,
I scaled their sighs, climbing
into their mouths with my broken
animal ways, having the nerve
to be angry when they spit me
into the curling dust.

A heartbroken poet is redundant.
Follow the balled-up odes that only hit
their mark after the leaving, when I remember
the taste of jambalaya kisses on her neck
the soap smell on her thigh,
the Great Morning After Omelete Debate of 2016,
the lifting hug, the quickened hush thrust,
the rasp of tongue that knows me better
than anyone, ever, again.

If it were not for the piercing between my ribs
I might mistake this for ecstasy.

Black Night is Falling: Sun Tzu

If it were not for the poetry,
I might mistake her for a religion,
her memory a holy ghost,
her lap a heaven of redacted love songs,
her kiss a terrifying and final revelation.

LAST ONE GIVEN

There was supposed to be a cleansing here,
where I got to see your thigh once more
curving back into you, where, to the uninitiated,
the waste becomes a shame.

The morning after I am left for dead,
my linen a shroud, my throat full of your grain.
I cannot tell if the sun is winter's or you.

I left a kiss on the watermelon lemonade of your skin.
You did not feel it. This does not offend.
After the tree I tattooed onto your back
with oil and spoon, there is no sensation left to offer.

It was kiss as garnish, that knew what was coming,
my lips pressing into the stump of your spine,
my chin grazing the engine of your walk.

The tree wearing you blooms now, but will fade.
Leaves will fall off of you first, then timber.
Only the roots, coiling around into your belly,
wrapping your breasts from behind, will keep ringing.

I never fought so hard for an ankle before,
the turn of a neck that makes a chic dance of your hair.
We were supposed to be clean by now.

Baptized in this glen of sheets and suckling
I did not even close my eyes when you set me under,
your arms dropping me into the water,
my skin a robe of old sins made new ones.

When you left, I went with you. I can feel the breeze
even now against the clove on your neck.
Every lover after this deserves our pity.

HOW POETS SAY THEY LOVE YOU NOW

Thesis in the contrary, preferably with dissonant resolutions. A conjunction of common acts. A couple of random suggestively violent acts. A couple of acts of soft character. A concrete affirmation of previous softness. A mundane act turned on its head by an unworkable detail. A contrary opinion on a generally accepted beauty. Mundane act. Mundane act with detail. Repeat. Mundane act cut with impossible cosmic implication, plus mundane act; spoiler: self-reference. Mundane act with pop culture reference. Mundane act that exposes subject's folly, drawn as a quote. Description of conspicuous behavior suggesting madness. Long line resolution with disparate mundane moments bookending contrary title with an emotion kicker.

SOUTHERN GAL

I have been too much to take in,
the hard swallow, a lurch of sea filling the gut
the glint of the last sun strobing overhead.
I take full responsibility.
I don't know how not to fill open spaces.
I rush in when breaking against rocks will do.
The stones always seem thirsty to me,
their cups curved just right for filling.
There are no atheists in the drink.

Those with un-casting hands, let us lift
our glasses to beaches, to stones and shells
and flotsam from other travelers who knew the way;
to mermaids who shined their smiles by day
and turned tail at the sign of rescue,
half truth, half fish, all tail.
Cheer the shores for keeping us in line,
us oceans of intention and depth,
shallow as the silt of small talk where necessary.

I only want to remember the sighs
the cracks of your toes in my ear
the cotton field of your scalp
the spider leg of pinkie in the air
when you drank me curling into your waiting lip.
The sun dies of shame
in the afternoon made of your swinging twists
and the cicadas trapped
in our bayou of a kiss.

AN ACT OF BLACK-ON-BLACK TIME

Let your coffee go cold staring into my face,
wondering how much of me is my mother
and how much is decisions.
Let me take the long way 'round to tell you,
it's 75 percent.

Ask me about my day, then interrogate me.
Wonder how much I puffed up at the white gaze
I shed that day, and how much I bemoaned
when it passed me by for smaller mouths.

Savor me. Treat me like a death row dinner,
like this moment couldn't possibly exist again.
Stare at me like more of me might reveal itself
in 3D, to the side, when the psychedelic me kicks in.

Do not disturb is not enough; let us destroy our phones.
Crush something hard under something soft for once.
Tell me how much you love poetry
and I will tell you how much I adore spectacle
and then we can raze a police station to the ground
with our performance poetry until we forget that,
no matter how many cops we've run into the street,
if the spectacle outshines the poem we have failed.

You beg me to stop you from going on too long
and I refuse. I know you are used to office spaces that
track your every frown and heavy sigh, a black demerit
against the credit score of your race.
I hope you take all of their staples and make
silver cubicle curtains with them.

Be a criminal with me, now. Let us steal away slowly,
our pockets full of time, minutes spilling out of our collars.
Kiss me on the expiration date in the nape of my neck.
We already been 'round longer than the label say.

HO'OPONOPONO

All I want to do is cook
in the kitchen of your hair,
simmer to the root.
But then, everybody takes shelter in you
while being a whole storm,
dragging they thunder all across
that sky in your mouth.

I told you the funniest joke I'd ever heard
and you hid your smile from me,
like trapping all that glissando actually works.
Turned your blue hip into the sun and autumn,
gave me the belly laughs you'd never shared
with anyone who didn't know the combination:

>   Left-Left-Sorry
>   Right-Forgive
>   Left-Left-Thank You
>   Click-Love

One afternoon I woke up from a dream –
a beautiful road trip concoction –
and realized that everything I did
only ever sent me in one direction.
Every job, every chore,
every paycheck, every whistling dance,
every leaf turned to angel's breath after death
raked into a sorrow engine and poems,
every mystery, every misspoken lyric,
every strum of a sunbeam
cut loose on your Socratic side-eye;
all I was ever doing was accumulating time,
and when I had enough of it, I'd spend it all
on lying here, cut grass living in my collar,
listening to the roar of an asphalt ocean,
my head in your sundressed lap.

Black Night is Falling: Sun Tzu

What else do I need but this religion?
What do I need to decolonize out of this kiss
to make it a worthy offering?
And if I know this is the answer –
the white noise fabric on your thigh in my ear –
then let us call out the hymn of your name
for the mantra it is because
that's where the freedom resides:

I should not get to stay unless I can make things right.
And so I am sorry.
I should not be allowed to remain until you say
And so I beg forgiveness.
I should not take you for granted.
And so I thank you.
I should not know parts of you if I cannot say the words out loud.
And so I love you.

And so I am sorry.
And so I beg forgiveness
And so I thank you.
And so I love you.
I'm sorry.
Please forgive me.
Thank you.
I love you.
I'm sorry.
Please forgive me.
Thank you.
I love you.

CAN'T LOSE
(RZA)

SMOKESTACK LIGHTNIN'

Universal maxim #3,742,946:
Thou shalt not use Howlin' Wolf songs
in commercials for erectile dysfunction.

The television screen fills with the lonely image
of a Daper Dan man out at sea, steering his sailboat
against the tide of nature and time, wanting and incomplete.
And there's Howlin' Wolf in the back,
blowing over Hubert Sumlin's gospel lick,
the perfect juke joint soundtrack for one man's quest
to reclaim his hard-on.

Perhaps I am seeing the commercial all wrong.
Maybe Viagra is the cure for white folks' blues.
Taken in that light, my advice changes dramatically
from cosmic poetic understanding to marketing strategy.

Ergo, if your goal is to cure white folks of the blues,
you should interrupt Howlin' Wolf with a snatch
of Twisted Sister at the end,
something that says, "Ah, my dick is awake,"
the kind of music a prick would sail a boat to.

WHEN ALL OF THE TALKING HEADS
IN THE BLUES DOCUMENTARY ARE WHITE

Pumpkin spice is considered by many
to be one of the greatest seasonings of all time.
I've spent the last 20 years studying the taste
and applications of pumpkin spice.
I became a scholar of pumpkin spice, but also
came to it as an eater, trying to get inside
understand what its state of mind was.

I read everything I could get my hands on,
consulted all the experts in the field:
Professor Pookie Brown Johnson the Third,
Professor O'Shea Miller Jackson Jones,
Tyrone.
Just a pantheon of brilliant pumpkin spice minds.

Because there wasn't much known about pumpkin spice,
it came with a little bit of mystery attached to it.
It was said to have been a novice condiment, not very good.
And then it came back and it was in everything:
lattes, Pop Tarts, pumpkin spice pretzel bites
Frosted Flakes, pumpkin spice cottage cheese
Just everywhere.

It is generally thought to contain a blend
of ground cinnamon, nutmeg, ginger,
cloves, sometimes allspice.
But in my extensive research I've discovered
that this recipe is largely untrue.
What we're really talking about is:
12 parts ground mayonnaise
4 parts tiki torch oil
3 parts pepper spray
3 parts white women's tears

Legend has it that the spice was taken

Black Night is Falling: Can't Lose

by a really woke pony-tailed yoga instructor,
who went down to the crossroads,
sold its essence to Anthony Bourdain,
and became the greatest powdered spice in the world.
Pumpkin spice is the template for every spice we use now.

It originally comes from the genteel microbreweries
of the late twentieth century but really,
Black people made it the spice it is now.
You wouldn't know this spice if it weren't for
the Baptist fish fry and pig feet keeping that tradition alive.

White people may have invented it,
but it's everybody's spice now.
I'll admit it's a little jarring to go to the cookout
and see no white people and all that gourd-scented love
but these things happen.
Sometimes a spice just infuses and moves on,
becomes something else, something we can all enjoy.
Sometimes a spice just finds a new audience
and the old audience just gives it up,
moves on to other seasonings.
Anybody is welcome to pumpkin spice if they can find it.
And if they find it, if they can afford it.
And if they can afford it, if they can find the meaning.
And if they can find the meaning, then they'll realize
that pumpkin spice belongs to everyone.

NONSENSE & REGULATION

Do you know why I pulled you over sir?
License and registration please.
Birth certificate and fingerprints, please.
Slave papers, please.
Pick and hoe, please.
Step out of the slave ship, sir.
Step out of the cellblock, sir.
Step out of your skin, sir.
Step out of line, please.

Keep your hands where I can see them, please.
Keep your plans where I can freeze them, please.
Keep your palms bleeding
from the stigmata of this electric cross, please.

Freedom papers, please.
Dental records, please.
Skin and bone, please.
Everything you own, please.

Can you walk this line, sir?
Can you work this row, sir?
Can you find the cotton we have hidden in your cubicle?
Can you find the daily shuck in that hourly jive?
Can you find your way to be one of the good ones?
Can you stay being the funny one in the office?
Can you unhinge your jaw for me, sir?
Can you speak the language I have provided for you?

Put your hands on top of the vehicle, please.
Put your child on top of this bush of cotton thorns, please.
Let their blood be the wine of gods that look like me,
that only love me, that only bless me, that only wear my colors.

Do you have any drugs in the vehicle, sir?
Do you have any weapons in the vehicle, sir?

Black Night is Falling: Can't Lose

Do you have any books in the vehicle, sir?
If I search the vehicle will I find that you have any contraband?
Any self-respect? Any shrines to ancestors we have pulled over before?
Will I find that you have already been to three funerals this year?
Will I find that you have mistaken a slogan for a life?

Will I find the brambles of the field in your collar
or will you smell of house biscuits and white meat?
Will I find I am blinded by all your teeth smiling when I pat your head
or will I discover that you can secretly read?
Will I then find my gun come to me now?
Will I have to? Will you make me?
Will you force me to kill you because I fear your shaking eyes?
Fear the tears falling from your argumentative mouth?
Will you force me to kill you because you refuse to put out a cigarette?
Will you at least litter so we can get this over with?
So that one of us can get home in time for dinner?

Do you know why I pulled you over?
Did you think I wouldn't because you're not a criminal?
Did you think I could tell the difference?
Did you think there was ever a difference?
Did you think the field ever left your armpits because
I gave you new dresses and belts for your pants while you're in my house?

Do you know why I pulled you over?
Did you know you were homeless before the house burned down?
Do you understand these rights that I have not stated to you?
Do you see where I have kicked holes in your drums?
Made do-rags of your runaway quilts?
Did you think the field ever left your nappy head
because you laid it to the side?
Did you think the field was out there somewhere?
Did you think the field was still over there?
Did you think we wouldn't figure out how to put a roof over that field?
Put some bars where the bushes stop?
Did you think we wouldn't think of that?
That if we ran out of land we'd run out of needing you?

Scott Woods

That's the biggest crime here, sir, what you don't know.
The field was never outside, and the house?
The house uses the whole world for floors.

THE CAR RUNS THE UNDERGROUND RAILROAD THROUGH BEXLEY, OHIO

(Apologies to Colson Whitehead)

If I am present and you are ever tempted to ask
the author of a surreal slavery novel what their upbringing was like,
by which you mean, where they make Black people like you,
I am obligated to sideswipe you with *The Car*.

When *The Car* came out in theaters for a whole six minutes in 1977,
it was the most terrifying thing all three of us had ever seen.
The premise was simple: a murderous, demonic vehicle
rips through the desert town of Santa Ynez for 96 minutes straight.

The Car was a 1971 Lincoln Continental Mark III black coupe,
to date the blackest car anyone has ever seen.
As the movie hired no Black people, *The Car* killed no Black people
and the enemy of my enemy is 27% on Rotten Tomatoes.

If you are tempted to point out that you once vacationed
in South America, and that you could see how being a minority –
for a little while – would be difficult, especially when
you have nowhere to go back to, you should know that the room
is wondering what the rock you have been under must weigh,

Four cars were built for *The Car*.
One for close-ups, the other three reserved for stunt work.
Two cars were destroyed while making the movie.
One car is fawned over daily in a private collection.
There is one car unaccounted for, left to the back roads of Saint Ynez.

The answer is, I was raised on Saturday morning cartoons,
Corn Flakes and buttered toast mash-ups on my tongue,
and a secret society whose core belief is that there is
an indestructible blackness on wheels out there,
afraid only of sacred ground, which must be why
you build your empires on so many cemeteries.

Scott Woods

Somewhere in the night, chrome so bright it feels
like two rows of teeth laid quick and scraping against the eye,
circling the coffeehouse outposts of a new gentry,
is a 1971 Lincoln Continental Mark III black coupe
that fishes for the well-meaning with a gospel
comprised of steel and the brave answers
to horrible questions.

THE SCOTT WOODS I HAVE NOT FRIENDED ONLINE

That Scott Woods is the fifth Scott Woods to send me a friend request.
That Scott Woods has three children, but clearly has a favorite.
That Scott Woods dresses up for Halloween, poses with his daughter of choice.
One year he is a werewolf, she a zombie of the *Monster High* variety,
which is to say she is no real zombie at all.
I posted about a *Twilight Zone* marathon, about police abuse.
It is physically impossible to pull that Scott Woods over.
He is blonde.
He is on a boat.
He was in the military and will never forget.
I am Black and scared of boats and chill at the sight of camouflage.
I forget so many things. Go out of my way to forget.

That Scott Woods loves sunsets, and this we have in common.
We do not see them from the same types of places.
He wouldn't know anything about climbing
a carryout dumpster to see the sun.
That Scott Woods has a tattoo on his left bicep.
I cannot tell what it is but it is old, the color running into
the pool water he is swimming in.
My entire life is tattoo.
My color never runs.
I do not swim, but not because my color runs.
That Scott Woods has at least one brother. They look alike.
I don't look like any of my brothers.
If we weren't related we wouldn't even know each other.
That Scott Woods looks like he would seek
his brother out for a beer and a boat and sunset.

That Scott Woods is in a group picture with thirty other people.
All of them are white.
It is a social setting.
I am unclear if that Scott Woods has any Black friends.
Perhaps this is why he sought me out.
I can make friends out of white people anywhere
because they are everywhere.

Scott Woods

Where that Scott Woods lives clearly has a dearth of Black people.
I might start with the Black people with my name too.
He likes his coffee like he likes his friend requests: black.
Except I am the only one on deck that I can tell,
so he may simply be black-curious,
and it is wholly possible that he is drinking tea
in a wholly inappropriate cup.

It takes me several pages worth of scrolls to uncover
that that Scott Woods lives in England.
Now everything is different and yet, exactly as expected.
Now that Scott Woods has an accent.
That Scott Woods is definitely drinking tea.
I thought that when he chided his friend Michael about
asking what time kickoff was that he meant football,
which is to say, my football.
We don't even have that in common.

I have looked up over 75 Scott Woodses on the internet in my lifetime.
All of them have been white.
I have never met any other Scott Woodses face to face.
This Scott Woods won't be the one that breaks the streak.
I may be the only Black Scott Woods in existence,
a dahlia hologram floating in an electric ocean,
picked in the wild by a me searching
for a version of himself that loves dead bluesmen
and bad barbecue, which I would feed him,
in that order, because we Scott Woodses
have to look out for one another.

DON'T SAY FRIEND

when you mean lover

when you mean co-worker

when you mean acquaintance

when you mean date

when you mean ex-lover

when you mean aunt I am no longer talking to

when you mean anti-politic

when you mean make no waves over this dinner plate

when you are all yes sir and no ma'am any other time

when you mean free therapist

when you mean safety net

when you mean convenience

when you mean secret

when it didn't rained that day

when the playlist changes when you aren't looking

when you mean trying him on

when you mean checking the fit

when you bad at it

when you transactional with it

when driving down one-way streets

when you vicarious with it

when you mean avatar

when you mean don't know where to put this heart so put it here, in this

when you mean please don't hurt me

when you mean sucker

when you mean mark

when you mean customer

when you mean acolyte

when you mean sycophant

when you mean winter is coming cuffing season

when you mean bridge I haven't burned yet

when you mean neither of us is going anywhere anyway

when you mean don't know what else to call you now

when you mean have you heard of our lord and savior Jesus Christ

when you mean how much do you currently pay on your electric bill

when you mean ATM

when you mean I'll pay you Tuesday

when you mean come on, brother

when you mean constituent vote ballot bullet

when you mean flyer under my windshield wiper

when you mean creep kept at bay

when you mean didn't mean to turn you on

when you mean please stop hitting me

when you mean guy who makes office coffee every day without complaint

when you mean service worker who cannot escape the gravity of your wallet

when you mean bookmark

when you mean chase me

when you mean I've lost myself and you look like a map

when you mean addiction

when you mean because I let you get away with this

Scott Woods

WHAT THE MEN YOU END UP WITH WILL POSSESS

newly pressed old vinyl, with matching pants
earrings like plates framing eyes like philosophy classes
a djembe he knows how to hit but not play

~~a prescient distaste of all of the poems you write~~
~~a passport without one ghetto stamp~~
~~rap music that even Black folks don't like~~

anywhere he just came from will be better than here
every book written by exactly five people
and then, just enough

IN SEARCH OF A CITY

1.
All of the city guides got it wrong:
streets is drums, not symphonies;
is grinder music, not song.
All that bus line backfire be swing, no soul.
Streets is backs to be beat on,
rhythm gliding along their cheeks,
too cold to hold time by themselves,
even in a killing summer.

My man sleeping on that park bench
thinks it's hilarious that anyone believes
the streets is where the soul of a city lives
while he lies there every day
brimming with so much love to give.

All of the city guides use our bones
to tell you where you should go, but
not our hearts.
Never where we dream.
Never how we live.
Make a circus of a city of the dead
that don't know it's gone.
You can get anybody to lie in a coffin
if the pillows are soft enough.

2.
No street got no job
'less someone got somewhere to go.
All the curb ball in the world
won't make your street game
if it ain't got no edge.
And that's what you are:
all midwestern road,
flattened hills
gray

all valley.
You don't even hold your black that long.
Tarred and weathered,
beat the black out with every trip
You a trip, city.

On streets, I have shred my knees
to kindling, kneeling to kiss your asphalt
as if it could love me back,
as if your job isn't to take whatever we give
on our way to something softer,
something that knows its way around
a tray of #5 peppered steak
or will speak to me about the Halle Berry
I used to love, anything that might kiss me back.

3.
All property is a façade.
Everybody keeps talking about architecture
like it means buildings.
Like it don't also mean
what ain't there no more.

All property is a façade, and
you can't build a city with the bricks of shame,
cannot lead with a politics of guilt.
As if we are not voting for your humanity
As if we are not pretending
that a city can have a living, breathing moment.

It is your civic duty to pretend you care,
and I, too, want to see the difference between
freedom and liberty someday.
Every time I have ever flipped a lever
I was hoping to be fed
even when I knew I was running
on a wheel in a cage.
You could fight me with your love

and I might let you win,
but you don't know anything about pulling punches.
You only know swing, and I only know
how to tell you that you're telegraphing your punches.

4.
A fight don't always feel like one.
You can just treat me like I'm not there.
A little erasure goes a long way,
will get the job done when a wrecking ball won't do.
Ravage all of my places like a sword swallower of worlds:
the barbershop that knew the crane of my neck,
the rib shack on 5th and 5th,
the secondhand shop with firsthand aspirations.

Having lost the Battle of the 92 Unloved Flowers and
the Skirmish of Heaven's Prodigal Sons,
you grew a gated community in my Franklin Park chest,
death by a thousand swing sets and flower beds.
Where can a soul find solace if the body stays under siege?
Where can a soul ever manifest
if the mind must die before knowing peace?

5.
Look now:
show me that thing you do
when no one is looking,
that way you embrace folks
like you love them until you mean it.
There are not enough Sunday mornings
between us yet for this love letter.
I admit I have only ever told you
what you are not, where your soul
could not possibly reside, but almost never
where it curls up whenever
your moon passes in front of my sun.

If I did not believe you had it in you

I'd already been gone.
You have an outer belt shaped like a heart
I cut my grass in your left ventricle;
So what if the heart of it all is not to be found
in the chest? What if it beats
in your serenade of well-meaning violins
in your art-shaped park that never turns autumn brown
in your smokehouse I dare you to eat at
in your shoe shop that will still sell you
a zoot suit in This Year of Our Lord
in your complex of blackberries
that is not complex at all
in your skyline of daggers that looks
like a lover's hips today
If I did not believe you had it in you,
I'd already been gone.
And yet here we are,
sitting across from one another,
waiting to see if the bones of truth
can ever be worth more than what lie
we can build on top of them.

PAUSE

Full off your soup of alphabet jokes,
served off all that fine gay china.
Should keep Bayard Rustin's name out your mouth.
Quit posting James Baldwin clips.
Stop telling me you adore the tragedy of Hansberry.
And while we're on raisins,
stop telling me Langston is your favorite poet.
And while we're on the music
to be found in a Black man's feet,
quit playing in my face about Alvin Ailey.
And while we're on the blues,
cease and desist your praise of Bessie Smith.
Quit praising Audre Lorde when you would salt
the doorstep as if she were infection.
Don't tell me you're proud of Marsha P. Johnson.
If you see Griffin-Gracy in the street, just keep moving;
it's what you want to do anyway.
Sashay past Willi Ninja, except you can't now.
Give back that whole renaissance you love,
that one you want every school to teach, but only so much.
Scratch a Harlem street too vigorously
and you'll catch it, you heard somewhere.
How you love and hate history at the same time?
How you okay with half a freedom?
How sway? And hip turn? And perfect twerk?
How tall the bars on this gate you keeping?
And who made them? Who held a steel rod to the embers
and then the anvil and beat its true form out of it?
Because I have seen your hands. Too smooth
for the kind of work we talking 'bout.
Best leave that job to folks who know
how to pull truth out of hot hells.

WE ARE SO CIVILIZED RIGHT NOW

It's really quite simple:
we can be civilized about this
or we can be human beings.
I don't know which of those is worse,
but experience tells me
there might not be a winner here.

Every civilized flick of the wrist
comes with its own blanket of bones
scattered rough into a crumbling crust
of inventions and oppressions
that can't wait to get to a dinner party.
Every human being
hiding a laundry list of sins
no one will ever know except the people
whose shirts they've dirtied,
whose knees they've stained.
You can't even get to human being status
until we've determined you're civilized.

So we can be civilized about this
or we can be human beings,
or we can be gods,
making up creation as we go, improvised livin'.
Every death a rough draft of some religion
we could have got right if we sat down
considered the civilized or human being parts.
Or
or we can be gods,
knowing everything, saying nothing,
a selfish cosmos.

Or
or
or we can be deadbeat gods
that cared enough to create all this

that one time, back in the day,
then walked away, satisfied with themselves,
dust collecting on our wars
as we sit on a shelf the size of a galaxy
waiting for our prayers to be answered,
a universe of tchotchkes,
a toybox the size of a planet
in a graveyard the size of creation.

We can be civilized about this
or we can be human beings,
or we can be animals.
Animals that know what they are.
Animals that have no agenda
that does not involve the cuisine of survival.
Animals that wouldn't know a bomb
if you gave them the codes
and wouldn't worry about which afterlife to pick
from the menu that animal chefs never design.
Animals that live every day like it's their last
because it is; animal never the same twice.
Not unless you civilize it.
Not unless you give it to a human being.
Not unless you make it hungry so you can watch it dance
Make it hungry so you can walk it the right way
Make it hungry so you can do anything to it
that isn't unto like animal.

And that is what we have done
to the animal both inside and outside of us,
and the human beings we are and pretend to be,
and to our gods who either know everything
or we pull fast ones on all the time.
We have civilized them.
Do they love us or have we conditioned every inch
of this existence?
We have made everything a circus trick.
We have made everything hungry.

We have made the very act of waking up
a brutal uncivilized religion.

LAND ACKNOWLEDGEMENT

We would like to begin by acknowledging that the land on which we gather here today is the occupied and unceded territory of a people's chipped and dying morality;

by acknowledging that we are in the ancestral nation of the doublespeak, of the original thought crime, of the bomb-while-you-eat platter.

The rolling valley of lesser evils where no sun shines between its agenda of hills, so we bulldoze and blast the sky until it gives up its ghosts.

We acknowledge this land of genocides, but only the old ones, the harmless histories that we have fracked into a new religion. The government approved genocides that, by virtue of government approval, aren't genocides at all. Or the very far away ones that look like ours but we are assured are not, and so we should sleep on that, a bomb for pillow.

We acknowledge a colonialism that circles my block like an August ice cream truck whose song is an anthem you can kneel to. A chocolate gentrification. A bomb pop in name and outcome. An erasure delight.

A land where anything is possible and yet no one is brave or free enough to prove it. We note that this land is empire eating itself, starting with my street, my children, my history that I can't talk about for fear of being sued into an oblivion where my history must live.

We acknowledge that the land on which we gather here today has been stolen a dozen times over, and will be stolen a dozen times more;

that we stand on a land that can offer too much truth at once, a crippling truth, a shrugging of a globe of truth from our spines, rolling it down our arms like a Globetrotter trick.

We would like to begin by acknowledging that calling out this land is not a goal. It is not supposed to be a balm or a salve. It is not supposed to be The Work.

What in The Land's name are you so happy about, so proud of?
What about the naming of this land is so precious to you that you can acknowledge it over and over and it change nothing?
Where is the shame in all this dust you are raising?
How dare you steal it again with your self-righteousness?

We acknowledge that if the rock don't hit you, don't holler. But when you stand on a pile of rocks like that, your flag whip-cracking in the wind, we may be gathered here today to stone you, taking back each pebble, one at a time, until we can just call the land by its name again.

THE COOKOUT

BYOB: Bring our own blackness
We already got the ice.

Everybody you was worried about being here ain't,
and anybody who would complain about the noise
already got a plate, so turn it up.

This that whole block smell
like dinner smoke.
This that fish fry where
Whiting jumped out pond onto plate.
This that Cherrywood kiss,
that pecan soul stain,
that mesquite that knows you
and your momma's name.
This that meat sweat flopping off
burnt ends onto cooling lips.
This that sugar with a pinch
of grape Kool-Aid in it for good luck,
That dark coal gone white coal
gone bone dust gone eternal flame
flickering in the night.
That baptism that dips you,
holding your nose, into a hot sauce religion,
This that liturgy, the one where
you lose your tongue speaking it.

A cousin and his girl argue,
but about their love,
accidentally invoking Marvin Gaye:
- I want you.
      - But do you want me the right way, Clarence?
     'Cuz I want you, but I want you to want me too.
Even the babies tilt their sippy cups for that one.
Porchlight speckled through willow whips
make them night-dappled,

their shadows a curtain of dark love.
They got blues all over them.
The night hit different when you got no shame,

no worries, no shuffle, no gun blast game
no transgression, no dishonor, no maafa ruin
no depression, no disrespect, no what you doing
no blame, no triggers, no blues unasked for
no games, no Adidas 'cross that bathroom floor
no nos, no maybes, no showing your teeth, no laughter
no picking, no swinging, no fruit trees, no masters

AND WHO. BROUGHT. THAT. SUNSET.
Who tore up they kitchen
for that mix of blood orange and gold?
Who brought they gods to the party?
We have line danced our way to the distant shore,
already made our beds in the upper rooms of this place.
The moon is the only one late to the party,
the stars her plus-one billion,
jumping into the Electric Slide
like they were there the whole time.
As if we would cut them out.
That's why we made the Slide:
so we could dance with our parents
without anyone telling anyone else anything
but "Here we are, together, my loves."

As we slide into the storm we make
with our limbs, no one told us we'd have to reclaim
our bodies at the door, full on the bounty
of food like love and love like real love.
We no longer fit ourselves.
Spirits, we transcend,
We have become so large we see ourselves
before and after, running such beautiful game,
every part of us sprouting a life of wings,
all-seeing spinning wheel angels of blackness

until the sun says good night
because he has to work in the morning.
And we wish him fare thee well,
because tomorrow?
All this joy gon' wear him out all over again.

NOTES

"The Ave", "Ho'oponopono" and "The Cookout" were originally a suite entitled BLACK ODES.

"Day of the Dead at Bushman's Carryout" was originally published in the anthology, *I Thought I Heard A Cardinal Sing – Ohio's Appalachian Voices* (Sheila-Na-Gig Editions, 2022). Yes, it is a real carryout.

"Muva Drum", "Swole" and "Peace B. Steele" are ekphrastic works based on the art exhibit, Contemporary Coloured Deluxe (2023) by artist Tiffany Lawson.

"Song for a Razor-Shaped City" is an excerpt from a longer version written for TedX Columbus.

"Fence Shrine #7", "We Are So Civilized Now" and "Mija Woos Forgetting" were commissioned by the Wexner Center for the Arts for the film series, Sonnets and Cinema (2024), which I also curated.

"Franklin Park" was originally part of a performance suite entitled 7 Villages (2024).

"A Symphony of Uncaring" was commissioned for a fundraiser gala produced by the Community Shelter Board in Columbus, Ohio.

"Any Poet Who Says No Is A Liar" was written during a work meeting in which I was certain nothing of note would be conveyed. Right before the meeting a co-worker randomly asked if I had ever had my heart broken, so the subject was fresh in my mind.

"*The Car* Runs The Underground Railroad Through Bexley, Ohio" is complicated. In 2016, author Colson Whitehead and I briefly exchanged tweets about the 1977 horror movie, *The Car*. When he came to Columbus for an author talk the following year, I mentioned the film again on Twitter and there was another playful exchange. The Q&A that followed his reading didn't allow for me to ask *The Car* questions (which I was absolutely prepared to do), but that was probably for the best, as the Q&A was a dumpster fire of privilege-based ignorance.

"In Search of a City" was commissioned as part of a larger musical performance with the Mark Lomax Trio by the Johnstone Fund for New Music (2021).

ABOUT THE AUTHOR

Scott Woods is a writer and event producer in Columbus, Ohio. Woods is the author of *Urban Contemporary History Month* (2016), *We Over Here Now* (2013) and *Prince and Little Weird Black Boy Gods* (2017).

He has been featured multiple times in national press, including appearances on National Public Radio. He is the founder of Streetlight Guild, a performing arts non-profit. A 2018 Columbus Foundation Spirit of Columbus Award recipient, as well as the Greater Columbus Arts Council winner of the 2017 Columbus Makes Art Excellence Award for his event series, "Holler: 31 Days of Columbus Black Art," Woods was named the first-ever "Face of Columbus" by Columbus Alive. He is the 2022 winner of the Press Club of Cleveland's Ohio Excellence in Journalism award for Best in Ohio Essay Writing, and was awarded "Best Columnist in Ohio" in 2023 by the Ohio Society of Professional Journalists.

He is the co-founder of the Writers' Block Poetry Night. In 2020 he won an Ohio Valley Regional Emmy Award for contributions to *A House That Cannot Fail*. In 2006 he became the first poet to ever complete a 24-hour solo poetry reading, a feat he bested seven more times without repeating a single poem.

www.scottwoodswrites.net